MW01601378

Why Creators Burn Out

(And Why I'm Still Here)

Copyright © 2025

All rights reserved.

This is a work of nonfiction. All characters and descriptions of events are the product of the author's imagination and any resemblance to actual persons is entirely coincidental. The information in this book expresses the author's views and opinions and does not necessarily represent the views of any organization.

First published 2025

TABLE OF CONTENTS

Intro

Hitting Rock Bottom

2010 marks the worst year of my life. My marriage was crumbling, and even though I had finally climbed the corporate ladder into a position I had worked so hard for, I looked around and realized this was not where I wanted to be. Maybe that explains why my marriage failed. I was hardly home. I missed my kids' birthdays, school celebrations, holidays, and even my own wedding anniversary.

I didn't realize it then, but I was on a downward spiral into suicidal depression, eating myself to death.

Maybe I was afraid to hit the ground if I jumped off a building. Maybe I was too much of a coward to pick up a blade. Maybe eating myself to death felt like the only way out. I weighed 126 kg with a 46-inch waistline, and that extra weight came with consequences. I was suffering from chronic gout arthritis; my joints were busted, especially my fingers. There were days when I couldn't get out of bed because my entire body was in pain. I couldn't sit, stand, or lie down for long. I couldn't bend my knees. Even driving to work felt like torture.

Yes, I had the material things I thought success meant. But is this what success looks like? Sacrificing everything for the chase?

Call it karma, fate, or life. One morning, as I lay there catching my breath, literally fighting for air, YouTube randomly recommended videos from Gary Vaynerchuk and Eric Thomas. Their no-filter, no-excuses truths hit me like a train. Something in me snapped awake.

I forced myself to get up. I told myself that I am still in control of my life.

The first thing I did was quit my job. That toxic, cancerous environment was not worth my life. The next was agreeing to a mutual separation from my ex-wife, with shared custody of my two daughters. After that, I started working on my health, losing weight, rebuilding my habits, reclaiming my life. I still keep a photo of my overweight self as a reminder of who I refuse to become again.

During those dark months, I was barely holding myself together. I downloaded Gary Vaynerchuk, Eric Thomas, Simon Sinek, and many others' videos, converted them into MP3 files, loaded them into my iPod, and played them on repeat daily.

On the bus, on the walk to work, before bed, during lunch breaks.

Their voices were the only thing keeping my mind from drowning.

I was rewiring my brain one sentence at a time.

Then reality hit: what am I going to do now? Bills don't pay themselves.

I started an employment agency. To run one in Singapore, you need a license. I failed the exam three times and passed on the fourth. The old me would've quit after the first attempt. But I pushed through. Six months in, I closed the business. Market demand didn't match my supply. I was desperate again.

So, I returned to the aerospace industry, but this time with a different mindset. I no longer cared about climbing any corporate ladder. I showed up, did my job, and went home to work on myself. People call it a side hustle; I dislike that term. You're either working on your future, or you're not. That simple mindset shift changed everything for me.

In 2013, I quit my job again to start a food business. And yes, it failed within six months. Between rental, utilities, ingredient costs, and trying to keep prices low enough for customers, I got crushed. Food and beverage is still one of the toughest businesses out there. I was devastated again, beaten but not defeated. I picked myself up and went back to a day job.

But something changed in me.

After enough failures, I finally found what I wanted to do for the rest of my life. In 2014, I kickstarted my content creation journey while working full-time. I posted my first recipe on Facebook and never looked back.

You might wonder why food?

As a kid, I loved watching my grandmother cook and bake. She would grind her own spice blends by hand and make soy milk using those huge stone grinders. Watching raw ingredients transform into something magical fascinated me. That memory stayed with me all my life.

I decided that cooking, teaching, and sharing food is what I want to do for the rest of my life. Gary Vaynerchuk's voice played a big part in that decision. You'll be hearing his name a lot in this book.

I didn't restart my life with confidence. I didn't know what I was doing. I had no plans. I started from zero, exhausted, ashamed, lost, unsure. But I made a decision. And sometimes a decision is enough to change a life.

I told myself that if I was going to live, I would live with intention this time.

Not drifting.

Not on autopilot.

Not letting life happen to me.

I would show up even on the days I didn't feel like it.

Even when no one was watching.

Even when no one cared.

That one decision is the reason I am still here today, still cooking, still sharing, still rebuilding myself page by page, recipe by recipe.

And everything you are about to read applies to any kind of content you want to create, not just food.

Chapter 1

Why Creators Burn Out

(And Why I'm Still Here)

Fun fact: I'm still working a daytime job.

Yes. After more than a decade of posting content online, after hundreds of recipes, thousands of photos, hours of editing, writing, cooking, cleaning, documenting, sharing, teaching, I still punch in and punch out Monday to Friday like everyone else.

And I'm not ashamed of it.

In fact, I'm proud of it.

Many "gurus" and "influencers" will tell you to quit your job, chase your dreams, take the leap. Sounds romantic. Looks sexy on TikTok. Perfect for views.

But practically speaking, you don't need to quit your job to start this journey.

If you have a job that pays your bills, keeps a roof over your head, and gives you health benefits, why would you throw that away for the fantasy of becoming a "full-time creator" overnight?

Be grateful that you even have a job supporting your dream. There are people out there unemployed, desperate, who would trade places with you instantly. If you hate your job because it's toxic, then leave and find another job. There are always other jobs. Most people don't leave because they're comfortable with the salary, the seniority, and the predictability.

Our lives are made up of billions of decisions we've made so far.

Your current life is simply the result of those decisions.

If you don't like where you are, then make different decisions.

But don't blame your job, your boss, your schedule, your luck, your past, or the algorithm for why you haven't started.

You're not stuck.

Another fun fact: this journey isn't a fairy tale.

Most people are chasing a fantasy. They watch others and think:

"He makes videos and earns money."

"She posts pictures and brands pay her."

"I can do that too."

Then they try.

And reality hits them hard.

Alex Hormozi said it best: most people live in a loop. They watch others create, think it looks easy, try it, realize it's hard, quit, and chase the next shiny idea. It becomes an endless cycle of starting, quitting, and restarting without building anything meaningful.

Content creation isn't "hard" because of the work.

It's hard because of the mindset.

You have to show up even when you don't feel inspired.

You have to keep going even when no one's watching.

You have to stand strong when people troll.

You have to create not for applause, but for meaning.

That's the part most people can't survive.

If you're reading this and still want to try this journey, listen closely: don't quit your job. Use your free time to create content. Let your job fund your dream instead of destroying it.

I work eight to five. Add travel time, and my day stretches six to seven. Yet I still find time after work to write, film, cook, bake, edit, and post. I dedicate entire weekends to content. And on top of all that, I'm a single parent to two daughters.

If I can do this tired, broke, frustrated, gout-ridden, heartbroken, and rebuilding from scratch, you can find one hour a day.

If you're waiting for "the right time," if you keep saying you're "too tired" or "don't have time," this is my respectful response: no excuses. If I can do it, you can too.

This journey is not about intensity; it's about consistency. Once you start, stay disciplined. Stay committed. If you want to talk about Ninja Turtles, talk about Ninja Turtles. If you want to talk about bicycles, coffee beans, movies, or plants, then do it. As Gary Vaynerchuk says, go Smurf it out.

Or in my words, we need to nerd it out.

The Real Reason Most Creators Quit

Most people quit because they're scared.

Scared of judgment.

Scared of looking stupid.

Scared of starting with zero.

They post one piece of content, someone laughs or criticizes, and they fold.

Game over.

It's not because it's hard.

It's not because they lack talent.

Why Creators Burn Out (and Why I'm Still Here)

It's not because they don't have the right camera or studio.

It's because they can't handle being unseen.

They post something and nobody reacts.

No likes. No shares. No comments.

Silence.

And that silence kills them.

I need you to understand this clearly: every creator you admire started with zero.

Jay Shetty.

Simon Sinek.

Gary Vaynerchuk.

And yes, me.

You will start with zero too.

If you're doing this for numbers, you're setting yourself up to lose. Numbers will never satisfy you. They always live just out of reach. If your goal is simply to "get big," close this book and rethink your why. Because this journey demands something deeper than clout.

I started in 2014 on Facebook with fewer than ten people on my friends list. I didn't do it for attention. I did it because I loved the craft.

Do I enjoy editing videos or writing my blog now? Honestly, no.

But I choose to do it anyway.

Just like blanching green vegetables before sautéing makes the dish better. It's tedious. You boil the water, blanch them, time them, plunge them into ice. Then wash extra utensils. I don't enjoy the process, but I do it because the end result is worth it.

Content creation works the same way.

If you chase numbers, validation, or attention, you will burn out fast.

The moment you start measuring yourself against others, joy quietly leaks away.

And joy is the energy that keeps creation alive.

Trolls Will Come

The moment you step into the public space, someone will hate you. Not because of you, but because your existence reminds them that they never started.

We will be criticized for doing something.

We will be criticized for doing nothing.

So, we might as well do what we enjoy.

If someone takes time out of their life to write a hateful comment about you, take the high road. Empathize.

That person is lost.

That person is hurting.

That person doesn't have meaning.

Don't fight back.

Don't lower yourself.

Move on.

I grew up in an era where if someone punched you, you spit the tooth out and fight back. These days, someone sees a mean comment and disappears for months. Stop letting strangers on the internet dictate your worth.

If someone has time to hate you online, something is broken inside them.

Empathize.

Move on.

Post again.

Drive Over Motivation

Obsession Over Passion

People love to say, "Follow your passion and you'll find motivation."

No. Stop.

Motivation is temporary.

Discipline keeps you alive.

You brush your teeth every day not because you're inspired, but because you understand the consequence of not doing it.

Your creative journey works the same way.

Show up.

Even when it's boring.

Even when it's quiet.

Even when nobody sees.

You are planting seeds in soil no one else understands yet.

Take Breaks, But Don't Quit

Burnout happens.

To me too.

There are days I don't want to cook, film, write, or talk to anyone.

Days I disappear for a week or two.

Days I wake up tired in my bones.

Resting is not failure.

Resting is maintenance.

Sit.

Breathe.

Disconnect.

Return stronger.

You're human, not a machine.

Take breaks. Touch grass. Watch a movie. Bake something comforting.

Recharge.

Gratitude Is the Only Real Hack

One of the biggest reasons I haven't given up is gratitude. Not the cliché kind. I mean being genuinely grateful for the journey itself.

Simon Sinek said cars need gas to reach a destination.

Just like life, we need money to survive.

But the purpose of a car isn't to have gas.

The purpose is to get somewhere.

Same with life.

The purpose isn't money or materials.

The purpose is your goals, your dreams, your calling.

I'll add this: take care of your car. Maintain it. Be grateful it still moves.

Metaphorically, take care of your body and mind.

Be grateful for your progress.

I've learned to find the good when things go wrong. It took me years. Mel Robbins' 5 Second Rule helped change that. When I feel frustrated or worried, I count down 5-4-3-2-1, then look for the good.

Burnt dinner? You learned something.

Video flopped? You still created.

Nobody noticed your post? Keep posting.

The fruit may or may not come.

The act of doing is already a gift.

Your Why

If you're here for fame or money, put this book down.

Go do something else. I will send you a refund.

But if something inside you refuses to die… if something whispers, "I have something to give"… then welcome. You're home.

This journey is not easy.

But it is real.

And real is worth fighting for.

If one day your passion shifts, good. Let it shift. You're allowed to evolve. You are your niche.

But whatever you choose, choose what makes your eyes glow, not what you think will get more views.

So start.

Start now.

Start with what you have.

Start imperfect.

Post. Learn. Adjust. Rinse. Repeat.

And remember:

You didn't come this far to only come this far.

Chapter 2

The Myth of the Algorithm Savior

As we ended Chapter 1 talking about numbers, let's talk about something that destroys more creators than anything else:

The belief that the algorithm is the reason you are not growing.

I say: fuck the numbers.

There is no magic timing.

No magic sound.

No perfect hashtag combination.

No secret "post at 7.18 PM on Tuesdays" hack.

People keep searching for a cheat code because they are afraid to accept the truth:

Your growth is built inside you, not inside the algorithm.

The algorithm changes every week.

Your purpose should not.

You cannot build a career by chasing trends.

But you can build a community by showing up with consistency and honesty.

Most people do not want to hear that.

They want hacks, shortcuts, and loopholes.

Not discipline, patience, and resilience.

It takes tremendous time, effort, and discipline to get into shape.

Content creation works the same way.

There is no shortcut.

The Algorithm Is Not Your Enemy

People say things like:

"The algorithm is suppressing me."

"The algorithm hates small creators."

"The algorithm is the reason no one sees my work."

None of that is true.

The algorithm is just a machine showing people what they already care about.

If your content is real, valuable, and meaningful, it will find the right people.

It may take time, but it will. Because real things always break through eventually.

What most creators really mean is:

"I want success faster than my skill is developing."

That is not the algorithm's fault.

That is impatience.

So instead of fighting the algorithm, feed it.

Feed it with your story.

Feed it with your experience.

Feed it with your personality.

Feed it with your curiosity.

Feed it with your perspective.

The algorithm favors consistency.

People favor authenticity.

You win by being both.

Serve the 10

Maybe you only have ten followers.

Good.

Those ten are not placeholders.

They are not a "small audience."

They are human beings who chose to care about you.

Serve them.

When I say bleed for them, I mean:

Show up like they matter.

Because they do.

Make content that teaches them, comforts them, entertains them, or helps them escape for a moment.

Make them feel less alone.

Make them feel seen.

If you move ten people deeply, those ten will eventually become one hundred.

And those hundred will become one thousand.

Not because of luck.

Not because you went viral.

Because of trust.

People share what moves them, not what impresses them.

Impressive content is forgotten.

Meaningful content is remembered.

Your Intent Is the Real Strategy

Every piece of content should have one clear intention.

Not:

"I hope this goes viral."

But:

"I hope this helps someone."

One is ego.

The other is service.

If you are reviewing TMNT's The Last Ronin, do not just summarize the plot. Anyone can do that.

Tell people how it made you feel.

Highlight the details others miss.

Talk about the pacing, the artistry, the emotion.

Point out the panels that hit you in the chest.

Create both:

A spoiler-free version

A deep-dive version

Depth creates connection.

Connection creates community.

Community creates longevity.

That is how you win.

Not with tricks.

With honesty.

Treat Followers Like Clients

If you ever decide to monetize, understand this clearly:

Your followers are not numbers.

They are people who gave you something priceless: their attention.

Time is the most valuable currency in the world.

Once spent, it is gone forever.

If someone spends their time on your content, they deserve sincerity in return.

Value can be:

A recipe that saves them money

A technique that improves their cooking

A review that prevents them from wasting cash

A laugh in the middle of a painful day

A reminder that they are not alone

A story that encourages them to try again

Affiliate links still work.

Not because of discounts.

But because of trust.

People do not buy products anymore.

They buy belief.

If they trust you, they trust your recommendations.

Protect that trust like your life depends on it.

Because your brand does.

The Real Algorithm

The real algorithm is not digital.

It is biological.

Human attention runs on emotion, curiosity, identity, story, and familiarity.

You do not win by gaming the system.

You win by being someone worth returning to.

Show up when you say you will.

Speak your truth even when no one reacts.

Give value without expecting applause.

When you do that, the real algorithm activates:

Word of mouth

Emotional memory

Connection

Retention

The algorithm might forget your name one day.

People won't.

Final Note for This Chapter

The algorithm did not build your dream.

You did.

It did not make you pick up the camera.

It did not make you rewrite a script.

It did not make you get back up after failing.

It did not make you keep going when no one was watching.

You did.

Stop worshiping a machine that does not even know you exist.

The algorithm owes you nothing.

Your purpose owes you everything.

Create for people, not numbers.

Create for meaning, not measurement.

Create because something inside you refuses to stay silent.

When you focus on the craft instead of the charts, the right people will always find you.

Always.

Here's something I want you to think about:

If every social media platform disappeared tomorrow—Instagram gone, TikTok wiped out, YouTube vanished, Facebook erased—I would still be excited to start again from zero.

I would still wake up and create.

I would still document my food.

I would still share what I learned.

I would still post, even if the new format was VR, AR, holograms, brain-to-cloud, whatever the hell the future brings.

Why?

Because the platform was never the point.

The creation is the point.

But most creators are one-dimensional.

They cling to one platform like a lifeline.

They refuse to evolve.

They do not try new formats, new styles, new technologies.

They stay trapped inside what is comfortable.

Comfort kills creativity.

Comfort kills adaptability.

Comfort kills careers.

Creators get comfortable with their follower count, their subscriber base, their routine, their one platform they "understand," and then they stop learning.

The moment you stop learning, you start dying creatively.

If TikTok vanished tonight, most creators would panic.

I would not.

I would just move.

Because if your identity is tied to a singular platform, you are not a creator, you are a tenant, renting your worth from an app.

A real creator can start anywhere.

Why Creators Burn Out (and Why I'm Still Here)

A real creator can rebuild anywhere.

A real creator evolves with the times, not against them.

If all the lights went out, if all platforms reset, if everyone was forced back to zero, the ones who truly love the craft would rise again.

Be one of them.

Chapter 3
Finding Your Why

In the previous chapter, I talked about your why.

And I will say it again because this part decides whether you will last three months or ten years in this journey.

If you are doing this for quick cash, or chasing follower counts, or hoping to get famous, then you need to rethink your why before you upload that first post.

I will repeat this metaphor:

There is something most people refuse to admit.

Money is fuel, not a destination.

The purpose of a car is not to own a full tank of gas.

A car needs gas to move, but the destination is the true point of the journey.

Life works the same way.

Money keeps you alive, stable, and functioning.

But the purpose of your life is not to collect money like collectibles.

The purpose is to go somewhere with it.

To create something from your own hands.

To express ideas only you can express.

To build something that did not exist before you.

To become someone you respect.

If your only aim is fast results, instant virality, quick dopamine, or sixty-second fame, you will not last. And it is better you put this book down and return to your routine job like everyone else.

Because the creator journey is not a straight escalator upward.

It is slow.

It is messy.

It is vulnerable.

And it is honest work.

Start With What You Love

Before you even pick up a camera, write a list.

Write down everything that genuinely sparks something inside you.

Things that make your eyes light up.

Things that make time disappear.

Things you can talk about for hours without trying.

Things you will still think about even when you're tired from work.

Your list can be anything.

Don't filter. Don't judge. Don't shrink your weirdness.

Maybe you want to be the internet's handy dad, teaching people how to fix taps and shelves.

Maybe you love Ninja Turtles so much that you want to discuss the comics, the movies, the symbolism, the psychology behind each turtle's personality.

Maybe you love gaming. Not to be a professional player, but to share reactions, humor, frustrations, wins, and stories.

It can be food.

Sports.

Travel.

Collectibles.

Plants.

Coffee.

Sneakers.

Stationery.

Cleaning hacks.

Origami.

Movies.

Comics.

Pokémon.

Anything.

There are endless worlds waiting to be explored.

And no one needs to approve your idea.

You do not need permission to begin.

You only need curiosity.

Because when you truly love something, you naturally work harder on it.

Love fuels discipline.

Love creates consistency.

Love makes you stay up late without complaining.

Start With What You Have

Let me tell you my own beginning, because people always assume I started with some studio setup or "nice gear."

I started posting recipes on Facebook in 2014.

I had no fancy kitchen.

No professional camera.

No editing laptop.

No lighting.

No tripod.

No microphones.

No knowledge.

What I had was simple.

A Samsung phone.

Natural sunlight from a window.

And the willingness to try.

My first photos were bad.

Not "oh, this is okay" bad.

They were flat, dull, badly framed, messy, lifeless bad.

But I still posted.

If a recipe failed but was edible, I ate it and wrote notes.

If it was horrible, straight into the trash can.

Failing did not stop me.

Embarrassment did not stop me.

When I did not know how to build a website, I sat down and forced myself to learn.

When I sucked at photography, I kept shooting until something inside me improved.

When I could not afford a camera, I recorded with my phone.

When I did not know how to edit, I watched tutorials, tried, failed, adjusted, tried again.

That is what real progress looks like.

Not giant leaps.

Not dramatic transformations.

Just small steps repeated daily until something finally clicks.

The road to any kind of mastery is made of thousands of tiny decisions.

Tiny steps.

Tiny improvements.

Tiny breakthroughs.

It is not glamorous, but it is real.

Perfection is not a goal.

Perfection is fear in disguise.

Perfection kills momentum.

Perfection kills creativity.

Perfection kills your desire to even begin.

Forget perfection.

Choose progress.

Ask Yourself: What Is Your Why?

Now we go into the real question.

Why are you doing this?

Why are you putting time, effort, creativity, thought, energy, and emotion into something that pays you nothing in the beginning?

Why are you filming instead of sleeping?

Why are you writing instead of scrolling?

Why are you skipping nights out with friends to work on your craft?

Why do you feel pulled toward creating even when it makes no logical sense?

There must be a reason.

And that reason must be simple.

Simple enough that a nine-year-old can understand it.

For me, my why is clear.

I am trying to get more people into the kitchen cooking and baking.

I want someone who thinks "I can't cook" to pick up a skillet, try, fail, try again, and eventually say, "I made this with my own two hands."

If I can spark that in even one person, I am satisfied.

That is my why.

That is enough.

Find your version of that.

Not a slogan.

Not a branding phrase.

Not a marketing angle.

A truth. Something your heart has been carrying for years.

Your Why Must Be Stronger Than Your Excuses

Because excuses will come.

Every creator will feel tired.

Every creator will feel overwhelmed.

Every creator will doubt themselves.

Every creator will feel invisible at some point.

Every creator will wonder, "Why am I doing this if nobody cares?"

This is the moment where your why becomes your compass.

If you do not have a why, you will break.

You will quit.

You will disappear.

If you have one, you will breathe, rest, regroup, and continue.

Motivation will not save you.

Passion will not save you.

Those two are temporary, emotional, short-lived.

They fade the moment life gets stressful.

You do not need motivation. You need direction.

You do not need passion. You need purpose.

I will say this again:

Obsession is stronger than motivation.

Drive is stronger than passion.

Your why is the engine.

Everything else is decoration.

A Final Thought for This Chapter

Your why is the root system of your creative tree.

If the roots are weak, the tree collapses when storms come.

If the roots are deep, the tree survives seasons.

Storms will come.

Silence will come.

Failures will come.

But creators who know their why do not quit.

They pause. They rest. They reflect.

Then they return stronger.

So before you film another clip, before you hit upload, before you buy anything, sit down and figure out:

Why do you actually want this?

Answer that, and you will last longer than ninety-nine percent of creators who quit before they even gave themselves a chance.

Chapter 4

Infinite Niches, Finite Energy

In the previous chapter, I asked you to list down everything that interests you.

Your hobbies. Your obsessions. Your weird fascinations. Your guilty pleasures.

Once you actually put that list down on paper, you start realizing something powerful:

There are endless things you could create content about.

Yet most people still get stuck.

Why?

Because people love to romanticize this journey.

They think content creation is about finding the "perfect" niche, the one magical topic that will unlock overnight success, fame, fortune, and a million followers.

But let's be honest.

There is no perfect niche.

There are millions of niches.

You are not stuck because there are no ideas.

You are stuck because you're scared to pick one.

Scared of choosing wrong.

Scared of wasting time.

Scared that your first choice will ruin your whole future.

Relax.

You're not signing a 30-year housing loan.

You're making content.

Just pick one.

Stop overthinking your starting point.

If you need to, do this literally:

Close your eyes, throw a dart at your list, and start talking about whatever it lands on.

Even if it is something extremely unsexy like spreadsheets.

You think spreadsheets cannot be a niche?

There are creators making six figures teaching Excel shortcuts. Entire businesses built on formulas, dashboards, automation, and data visualization. And yes, one man literally built an empire explaining pivot tables.

His name is Chandoo.

He started with a simple blog about Excel. No hype. No flashy branding. Just real, practical teaching. Formulas. Reports. Data logic. Pivot tables. The kind of stuff most people fall asleep just thinking about. Yet he turned that into global recognition, premium courses, conferences, software tools, and a massive international community.

He didn't make Excel sexy.

He made Excel meaningful.

He proved something brutally important.

Why Creators Burn Out (and Why I'm Still Here)

It was never about the topic.

It was always about the depth.

It was always about how far you are willing to go.

And here's the part that still blows people's minds:

There is literally a world championship for Excel.

A real global competition where people compete live on stage solving spreadsheet challenges under time pressure. Speed. Accuracy. Advanced formulas. Data modeling. Strategy. Commentators breaking down decisions. Spectators watching like it's chess or Formula One.

The same Excel people complain about using at work… became a competitive sport.

Let that sink in.

If spreadsheets can become a world-class competition, your niche is not too boring.

Your approach might be too shallow.

Depth turns ordinary into extraordinary.

And Chandoo is living proof of that.

He didn't succeed because Excel was trendy.

He succeeded because he showed up.

Every day.

With clarity.

With generosity.

With consistency.

The niche never made him powerful.

Why Creators Burn Out (and Why I'm Still Here)

He made the niche powerful.

Topics do not create creators.

Creators create meaning inside topics.

Take J Perm, the Rubik's Cube guy.

A plastic toy became his full-time career.

He teaches solving methods, finger tricks, algorithms, and millions watch—not because of the cube, but because of him.

Again, the niche didn't create the creator.

The creator shaped the niche.

There are even creators who turned pen-spinning into an art.

The thing bored students do in class?

They made tutorials, challenges, competitions, and now they have communities, sponsors, and opportunities.

All from twirling a pen.

And then you have Adam Ragusea.

No fancy studio.

No restaurant kitchen.

Just a normal home kitchen, simple lighting, and an honest teaching style.

But he built a massive audience by being clear, curious, and human.

Or take Outdoor Boys.

A father documenting simple outdoor survival trips with his family. Camping in the snow. Cooking over fire. Teaching his kids basic skills. No flashy edits. No manufactured drama. Just real life, patience, and quiet competence.

At the height of his popularity, when the views were massive and the algorithm was fully on his side, he chose to step away.

Not because he failed, but because he knew when enough was enough.

He chose presence over pressure. Family over fame. Life over numbers.

And that decision alone says more about success than any viral milestone ever could.

This is the truth beginners ignore:

Topics don't create creators.

Creators make topics interesting.

It is never about the niche.

It is always about the person.

You are your niche.

Your voice.

Your style.

Your energy.

Your curiosity.

Your worldview.

Your personality.

Your life experience.

That is what people connect to.

Start With What You Can Do Today

Not tomorrow.

Not "when I buy better gear."

Not "when life is less stressful."

Today.

Turn your phone around.

Open your laptop.

Record your screen.

Talk.

If your house is noisy (like mine), mute the video and do a voice-over later.

If your background is ugly, face a window.

If your space is small, film tight shots.

If your equipment is limited, work with what you have.

You already carry a camera that films in HD or 4K.

You already have editing software, and if you don't, there are free ones everywhere now:

CapCut

DaVinci Resolve

InShot

In 2014, I didn't have these.

I struggled.

I learned the hard way.

You don't have the same excuse.

If you don't know how to use the tools, remove your ego.

Search YouTube.

Google it.

Ask ChatGPT.

The answers are all out there.

The only real difference between those who create and those who don't is this:

One person hits upload.

The other doesn't.

That's it.

That's the whole secret nobody wants to hear.

Experiment and Pivot — Without Running Away

Let's say you pick spreadsheets.

You post seven videos.

Then you realize:

"Bro… this is boring. I hate this."

Good.

That means you learned something.

Now switch.

Try another niche from your list.

But here's the part most beginners mess up:

Do not disappear.

Do not delete your account.

Do not ghost your audience.

Do not reset your page because it looks "messy."

"Messy" is human.

"Messy" is honest.

"Messy" is real.

Just post a simple update:

"Hey guys, after trying spreadsheet tutorials, I realized my heart isn't in it. I'm switching to talking about old-school comics instead. Thanks for sticking around."

Done.

Clean.

Human.

Real.

People respect honesty more than perfect branding.

And trust me, you only "find your niche" after trying multiple things, not before.

You cannot think your way into a perfect direction.

You can only test your way into one.

Every Platform Is Just a Tool

Beginners always ask:

"Which platform is the best for growth?"

The answer?

All of them.

YouTube

TikTok

Why Creators Burn Out (and Why I'm Still Here)

Instagram

Facebook

Pinterest

Threads

X

Reddit

Discord

Twitch

Blogs

Podcasts

Snapchat Spotlight

Funny thing is, almost nobody talks about Snapchat Spotlight, yet the organic reach there is insane.

Every platform works.

Every platform has creators making a living.

Every platform has potential.

Platforms rise and die all the time:

Vine — gone

Musical.ly — transformed

Facebook Pages — dead reach

TikTok — might get banned tomorrow

YouTube — unpredictable every year

If one platform dies tomorrow, your identity should not die with it.

Your creativity should outlive any app.

This is why you should spread yourself, not blindly, not recklessly, but strategically.

Be present in a few places.

Make your message larger than the platform.

Start Simple, Not Superhero Mode

Stop thinking you need gear.

You don't.

You don't need a podcast mic.

You don't need a lighting setup.

You don't need a camera that costs three months of rent.

Your phone is enough.

You want to start a podcast?

Put your phone on the table, flip it downward, and talk.

You want to shoot cooking videos?

Prop your phone with a cheap tripod.

Shoot overhead.

You want talking-head style videos?

Stand beside a window.

Natural light is the best light on earth.

You don't need gear.

You need courage.

You need repetition.

You need willingness.

That is the real starter pack.

So What Is the Real Point of This Chapter?

The point is simple:

There is no shortage of niches.

There is only a shortage of courage.

You're not lost.

You're scared.

You're not confused.

You're hesitating.

You're not lacking ideas.

You're lacking commitment to the first step.

Your niche won't reveal itself while you're thinking.

It will reveal itself while you're creating.

And once you start, you'll naturally gravitate toward the thing that feels right.

The thing that feels like "you."

The thing that doesn't drain you.

You will pivot.

You will adjust.

You will discover.

But you must begin first.

A Closing Reminder

You are not behind.

You are not late.

You are not too old.

You are not too inexperienced.

You are not underqualified.

You are simply at the beginning, and beginnings always feel confusing.

Start messy.

Start small.

Start scared.

Start with shaky hands.

Start with weak ideas.

Start even if no one watches.

But for your own sake, just start.

Because your niche isn't something you "find."

It's something you build with your own two hands.

Chapter 5

Slow Growth Is Still Growth

I have said this again and again in the previous chapters, but let me hammer this into your head one more time:

Every single creator on this planet started at zero.

Zero followers.

Zero views.

Zero attention.

Zero momentum.

Zero proof that this would ever work.

That includes me.

When I first posted on Facebook in 2014, the only people who saw my content were the handful of friends on my list. And when I say "handful," I mean less than ten people. Ten. That's it.

No audience.

No strategy.

No social proof.

No algorithm boost.

No encouragement.

Just ten human beings.

And you know the funniest part? I wasn't even active on social media before that. I didn't own a smartphone. I was walking around with a five-year-old BlackBerry that looked like it had survived a battlefield. No fancy camera. No editing software. No lighting equipment. No content plan. No analytics. No idea what I was doing.

But I posted anyway.

Not because I expected to blow up.

Not because I thought it would go viral

Not because I was chasing fame.

I posted because something inside me wanted to share. I posted because my "why" was louder than my fear. I posted because the act of creating itself felt meaningful.

Most of the time, nobody was watching. Nobody cared. Nobody commented. Nobody shared. But I still showed up. Slowly. Quietly. Repeatedly.

That is what real creators do.

Most creators quit long before they ever touch consistency. They see their numbers stagnate and immediately blame everything except themselves:

"The algorithm hates me."

"My niche is too saturated."

"I'm not early enough."

"My content isn't good enough."

"People don't care."

They blame, and blame, and blame, but they never look inward. They see the summit of the mountain, but they do not want the climb. They want the view without the bruises.

Why Creators Burn Out (and Why I'm Still Here)

The truth?

The algorithm did not fail them.

They failed themselves.They quit before the seeds had time to sprout.

My growth was slow. Painfully slow.

Let me give you real perspective. I only started taking Instagram seriously in 2019. After six years, I have just over ten thousand followers. TikTok? Same. YouTube? After years of posting videos, I barely crossed three thousand subscribers.

Do you know how many people would have quit long before that?

Do you know how many would have declared themselves failures?

I didn't. Because I never built for numbers. I built for people.

If I had ten followers, I bled for all ten.

If I had fifty, I gave my all to those fifty.

If I had one comment, I treated it like a conversation, not a statistic.

Every recipe I posted was for them.

Every caption I wrote was for them.

Every experiment I filmed was for them.

And here's something most people won't do:

I replied to every single comment. Every DM. Even when it felt overwhelming. Even when I was tired. Even when the comments were rude. Even when people were being trolls. I still replied with empathy.

Why?

Because behind every comment is a real human being. Someone took the time to type something under your post. The least you can do is acknowledge their existence. Attention is not owed. It is earned and returned.

People love to say, "If I only had more followers, I'd work harder."

No. If you don't work hard for ten, you don't deserve ten thousand.

Slow growth doesn't mean no growth. It means real growth.

Comparison is the thief of joy and the assassin of patience.

People compare their Chapter 1 to someone else's Chapter 70 and then wonder why they feel like they are losing. They look at massive creators today and forget the years they spent talking into the void.

They see Simon Sinek today on global stages with bestselling books and forget he spent years refining his ideas, speaking to small rooms, writing, and teaching long before anyone paid attention.

They see Gary Vaynerchuk today with global influence and forget he uploaded hundreds of Wine Library TV episodes before anyone outside his industry noticed.

They see Steven Bartlett today with one of the biggest podcasts in the world and forget that he started talking to himself in 2017 when literally no one was listening.

You see the highlight reel. You don't see the obscurity.

When you compare your beginning to someone else's peak, you will always feel behind. And feeling behind leads to quitting.

Slow growth protects you from that illusion. It forces you to earn every inch.

You want to know who I admire deeply? Chef John from FoodWishes.

Chef John taught me everything about patience without ever teaching me directly.

That man has been posting the same style of videos for over a decade. Same intro. Same voiceover. Same dry humor. Same consistent uploads. Same commitment to the craft.

He doesn't chase trends.

He doesn't panic about algorithms.

He doesn't rebrand every two weeks.

He doesn't beg for virality.

He simply shows up.

That consistency built him millions of followers. But that took years. Not months. Not weeks. Not hacks.

That's the difference between creators who last and creators who crumble.

The ones who last understand that this is a marathon, not a sprint. The ones who crumble are obsessed with shortcuts, hacks, viral moments, and instant validation.

But here is the uncomfortable truth:

You are not entitled to quick success.

Nobody owes you attention.

Nobody owes you engagement.

Nobody owes you growth.

You earn it

One post at a time.

One connection at a time.

One person at a time.

Patience versus ambition is the battle that makes or breaks creators.

Ambition is wanting everything right now.

Patience is understanding that everything takes time.

Both matter. But most people only have ambition and zero patience. They want results before they earn roots.

Yes, I am ambitious.

Yes, I want to grow.

Yes, I want my work to reach more people.

But I am also patient. I accept that this might take me years. Maybe decades. And that's okay.

Patience builds longevity.

Ambition without patience builds burnout.

Micro vs Macro

Micro versus macro is the real mindset shift.

Micro is what you do every day.

Macro is what you dream of long-term.

Micro looks like:

- Responding to comments

- Learning new skills

- Posting even when it's quiet

- Practicing when nobody is watching

- Improving inch by inch

Macro looks like:

- Building a personal brand
- Creating long-term opportunity
- Inspiring people
- Crafting a life that aligns with your values

Most creators fail because they only dream macro and ignore micro.

You cannot dream your way to success. You climb your way there.

If you have five followers, bleed for them.

Show up for them.

\Learn their names.

Reply to their messages.

Serve them harder than you'd serve five million.

Those five become your foundation. Your early believers. Your first real community. They carry your name into rooms you've never stepped into.

People forget this: early followers are not placeholders. They are pioneers.

I know creators with one hundred thousand followers and no loyalty. And I know creators with five hundred followers and an army.

The difference is depth, not width.

Slow growth builds strong roots.

Fast growth looks amazing. It is loud. It is exciting. It is seductive. But it is also fragile.

Slow growth is quiet. Boring. Unsexy. But it is bulletproof.

Imagine planting a tree. If it grows too fast, it collapses. If it grows slow, the roots go deep.

Your creative journey follows the same law.

Slow growth builds:

- Strong values

- Strong craft

- Strong identity

- Strong resilience

- Strong audience bonds

- Strong self-trust

Consistency beats everything else.

Greg Plitt said it best:

"The heart of a champion is a light switch that is always on. It doesn't go on and off depending on who's watching. It's constant."

That quote lives in my head because that is exactly what content creation is. A constant. You show up even when nobody sees you. You show up even when the results are invisible.

Consistency beats talent.

Consistency beats motivation.

Consistency beats algorithms.

Consistency beats everything.

Slow growth builds character.

If you grew overnight, you wouldn't be ready for it. Slow growth shapes you quietly into someone who can actually handle attention when it comes.

Slow growth teaches:

- Patience

- Grit

- Emotional control

- Craft mastery

- Focus

- Discipline

- Humility

- Gratitude

Every quiet post is training.

Every low-view upload is conditioning.

Every unseen effort is strengthening your foundation.

You want proof slow works? Look at me.

I didn't blow up.

I didn't go viral.

I didn't become famous.

But I built something real. Something authentic. Something sustainable.

People think I'm a full-time creator. I'm not. I still work a day job. I still commute. I still plan shoots around work hours. I still edit videos on public transport. I still write after dinner. I still juggle my daughters' lives with mine. I still deal with health struggles. I still deal with financial pressure.

But I show up.

I show up because I believe in what I'm building. I show up because I love this. I show up because someone out there needs to hear what I'm sharing.

Slow growth is still growth. And growth is enough.

This journey will test you. Stretch you. Frustrate you. Humble you.

But slow progress is still progress.

One follower is still a human being.

One comment is still a real connection.

One post is still a step forward.

One day, you will look back and realize every tiny step mattered. Every failure taught you something. Every quiet season shaped you. Every small win kept you moving.

Slow growth builds creators who last.

And I would rather last slowly than rise fast and vanish.

Chapter 6

Burnout Isn't Failure, It's Feedback

Burnout is not failing.

Burnout is your body speaking a language you have been ignoring.

Burnout does not arrive with fireworks. It does not knock loudly at the door. It starts as a whisper. A quiet resistance. A small sigh when you open your laptop. A hesitation before you press record. A delay before you reply to that comment. A tiredness that sleep alone cannot fix.

Burnout is not weakness.

Burnout is not laziness.

Burnout is not inconsistency.

Burnout is feedback.

It is the nervous system telling you that you have been running faster than your soul can keep up with. It is the body pulling the emergency brake when the mind refuses to slow down. It is the price of carrying invisible weight for too long without putting it down.

Resting is not failing. Resting is recalibration. It is stepping back far enough to see how far you have actually come. It is disconnecting in order to reconnect. It is pausing long enough to remember that you are not a machine built for infinite output, but a human designed for rhythm.

I live inside three full-time roles.

Why Creators Burn Out (and Why I'm Still Here)

My daytime job.

My content creation journey.

And being a single parent to two daughters.

So if anyone understands burnout, it is me.

There are days when I wake up and the idea of doing anything feels heavy. Not work. Not cooking. Not baking. Not writing. Not filming. Not editing. Nothing. There are days when I just want to disappear into bed and let the world pause without me.

Fun fact. Yes, I feel burnout. I always have. I am not steel. I am not wired differently. I do not possess some mythical motivation gene that makes fatigue bounce off me.

I simply learned to listen to the signals instead of fighting them.

And so can you.

Most people believe burnout happens to the weak. That disciplined people are immune. That "real hustlers" push through no matter what. That might look heroic on Instagram, but in real life it leads to collapse, not growth.

On my burnout days, I stay in bed until early afternoon. I game. I binge series. I drink coffee under my blanket. I escape into fictional worlds for a while. Sometimes I go to the theater. Sometimes I eat burgers at Five Guys (not sponsored). Sometimes I leave my phone untouched for hours. And sometimes, I disappear quietly for two full weeks without posting a single thing.

No announcement.

No apology.

No public breakdown.

Just rest.

And I come back.

Why Creators Burn Out (and Why I'm Still Here)

Because I understand something most creators do not.

You don't lose momentum by resting.

You lose momentum by lying to yourself that you are fine when you are not.

Burnout happens to everyone. Especially creators.

Content creation is not just mechanical labor. It is emotional labor. You are not just scheduling tasks. You are offering pieces of your mind. Your humor. Your ideas. Your failures. Your taste. Your identity. Every day. For public consumption.

That costs energy.

And that energy is invisible.

You don't just film a video. You think about it. Plan it. Doubt it. Script parts of it in your head. Worry about reception. Edit it. Rewatch it. Critique yourself. Compare it. Publish it. Check the response. Interpret silence. Interpret comments. Internalize feedback. Ignore trolls. Respond to kindness.

That's not "just posting."

That's psychological output.

Creators do not burn out because of work volume alone. They burn out because of invisible pressure.

Pressure to be consistent.

Pressure to grow.

Pressure to not fall behind.

Pressure to be relevant.

Pressure to stay inspired.

Pressure to monetize.

Why Creators Burn Out (and Why I'm Still Here)

Pressure to please.

And the heaviest pressure of all:

Comparison.

As I said in the previous chapter, comparison quietly robs you of joy.

It distorts your sense of progress.

It shortens your patience.

It blinds you to how far you've already come.

You compare your behind-the-scenes to someone else's highlight reel and start wondering why you feel exhausted, discouraged, or inadequate. But look closer and you'll notice the same illusion everywhere.

You are measuring process against presentation.

Instead of comparing yourself to who you were yesterday, you scroll into someone else's success and judge your unfinished work. You see numbers without seeing years. Results without seeing sacrifice. Explosions without seeing the long, quiet fuse burning in the dark.

You see the destination.

You miss the decades.

Comparison compresses time.

It erases the long middle.

And when the middle disappears, your own journey feels slow, broken, or pointless.

But it isn't.

You are not late.

You are not failing.

You are not behind.

You are simply in the part of the story that nobody applauds.

And that is where most meaningful work is actually built.

You never see:

- The breakdown in the shower
- The panic before uploading
- The months of silence
- The fear behind the confidence
- The exhaustion behind the smile

You only see the polished outcome.

Creators burn out because they try to replicate viral success instead of building identity. They try to reverse-engineer fame instead of forward-engineering meaning. They chase trends that do not belong to them. And when the trend ends, they are left empty.

Burnout does not begin with overwork.

Burnout begins with self-betrayal.

Burnout isn't caused by doing too much. It's caused by doing too much of what no longer feels true.

You start doing things that no longer feel aligned. You start posting things that no longer feel yours. You start creating for reactions instead of expression. And slowly, your soul stops recognizing the work.

If you feel burnout, do not panic. Burnout is not the end. Burnout is a checkpoint.

It is the moment your system says:

"Stop. Something is misaligned."

Take a breath.

Step back.

Recalibrate.

You are not quitting.

You are correcting course.

Now let's talk about hustle culture for a second.

We are surrounded by "motivational influencers" who glorify suffering without context. Cold plunges. 5am wake-ups. Perfect routines. Strict diets. Endless grind montages. Cinematic music. Perfect lighting. Perfect timing.

Ask yourself this.

Who set the camera up?

No one films discipline accidentally. That is a production. Not a life.

No normal human being wakes up camera-ready. Nobody smiles naturally at 5am. Nobody ice-bathes daily without questioning their sanity at least once a week. And even if someone does, that is their nervous system, not yours.

Their ritual does not have to be your religion.

My morning ritual is simple. A cold shower. The motion of grinding coffee beans to pulling an espresso shot. That's enough to reset me. That's what works for my nervous system. That's what brings me back into my body.

Your morning ritual might be:

- Running

- Journaling

- Cooking

- Long walks

- Long showers

- Quiet music

- Loud music

- Silence

Rituals do not need to look aesthetic. They only need to restore you.

Burnout is not the enemy. Avoidance is. Denial is. Pretending you are fine when you are drowning is.

Your body whispers long before it screams. The problem is most people only listen when it screams.

You are allowed to:

- Take a break without quitting

- Rest without losing momentum

- Pause without falling behind

- Step away without abandoning your dream

Burnout is simply your internal compass recalibrating direction.

It is not a stop sign.

It is a steering wheel.

And if you listen properly, burnout will not break you. It will evolve you.

You don't need to prove anything today. If all you did was survive, that counts. If all you did was rest, that counts. The work will wait. Your body won't.

Chapter 7

Reinventing Without Losing Your Soul

Reinventing yourself is part of the journey. Losing yourself is not. There is a difference. A big one. And this chapter is about protecting that difference.

When I say reinventing yourself, I do not mean selling your soul. Reinvention is growth, adaptation, curiosity. Selling out is abandoning your values for cash or fame. Reinvention is changing how you execute. Selling out is changing who you are.

In this journey, you will evolve.

But you should never erase the foundation that made you start.

That is why I always say this clearly:

Do not be a sellout. And remember your why.

As your content starts gaining traction, as your personal brand grows, offers will start coming in. Sponsorships. Collaborations. Affiliate deals. Free products. Paychecks. Shiny opportunities that look like success wrapped in good lighting and a contract.

Or maybe not.

Maybe your inbox stays empty for years.

That is fine too.

What matters is this: whenever the offers come, stay grounded. Stay honest. Remember where you started, how you started, and why you started.

I have turned down offers from huge corporations. Big labels. Well-known brands. Companies that would have made my bank account breathe easier. You know my medical bills. You know my responsibilities. You know how tight life can be. And still, I said no.

Why?

Because alignment matters more than relief.

A lot of people think that is foolish. They ask why I would not just take the money and secure myself financially. They assume integrity is a luxury only rich people can afford.

They are wrong.

The real cost of selling out is not external.

It is internal.

Selling out creates cognitive dissonance. You start justifying things you know are wrong. You rehearse excuses in your head. You tell yourself, "It's just one post." "Everyone does it." "I'll be more selective next time."

But next time comes faster.

And after that, faster still.

Soon, you are no longer creating freely. You are pre-editing yourself before brands even ask. You are second-guessing your honesty. You are shaping your voice around what sells instead of what feels true.

The most dangerous thing about selling out is not losing your audience.

It is losing trust in yourself.

I will give you a few examples of the kinds of deals I rejected.

A huge food brand offered me good money to promote their instant paste. The paste tasted terrible. I would not feed it to my daughters. I would not serve it to friends. So I said no.

A beverage company wanted me to hype their new "healthy drink." I read the label. The sugar content alone made my gout scream. Declined.

A cookware brand offered sponsorship if I demonstrated their "non-stick" pans. I tested them. Food stuck worse than my life in 2010. I walked away.

An overseas meal-prep company wanted me to pretend I used their service regularly. They even sent a script. They did not want honesty. They wanted acting. I declined.

These were not small deals.

Some were four figures.

Some were five.

Some would have helped.

But ease is not worth erosion.

Reputation is greater than money.

Always.

Ask yourself this honestly:

What legacy are you trying to leave behind?

Because the moment you start saying yes to things you do not believe in is the moment you start betraying your future self.

Yes, I do restaurant reviews.

Yes, I do product reviews.

But I only share what I genuinely believe is worth sharing.

I have never taken money from local food businesses for reviews. I know how hard they struggle. I will not exploit that just to sound generous on camera.

Let me give you one of my favorite examples of integrity at scale.

VLC Media Player.

You've used it.

Everyone has.

It plays everything.

It runs on everything.

It asks for nothing.

No ads.

No subscriptions.

No upsells.

No "premium" version.

Just a tool that works.

VLC was created in the late 1990s by a group of students at École Centrale Paris, led by Jean-Baptiste Kempf, Hugo Beauzée-Luyssen, and Rémi Denis-Courmont. It started as a dorm-room project. Students wanted a way to stream video across their campus network. That's it. No startup pitch. No venture capital. No growth hacks.

Just a problem that needed solving.

As the software grew, something rare happened.

They refused to sell their soul.

They kept VLC open-source.

They kept it free.

They kept it cross-platform.

Windows.

macOS.

Linux.

Android.

iOS.

They didn't lock users into ecosystems.

They didn't chase ads.

They didn't harvest data.

And yet, VLC became one of the most downloaded media players in the world.

That's reinvention done right.

The interface evolved.

The codecs expanded.

The platforms multiplied.

But the core never changed:

Give people a powerful tool without exploiting them.

They could have monetized aggressively.

They could have sold user data.

They could have crippled features behind paywalls.

They could have cashed out.

They didn't.

And because of that, VLC earned something more valuable than money:

Trust.

People install VLC without fear.

Schools use it.

Hospitals use it.

Governments use it.

Millions rely on it daily.

That's what happens when you protect the core while evolving the surface.

VLC proves this:

You don't need to betray your values to reach the world.

You don't need ads to scale.

You don't need to sell out to succeed.

You just need to solve real problems and stay honest as you grow.

That is reinvention without losing your soul.

Sadly, many creators do not care.

They take whatever pays.

They praise what deserves criticism.

They promote things they secretly dislike.

Then they wonder why their audience stops trusting them.

If you lose trust, the game is over.

Your integrity is not a personality trait.

It is an asset.

Protect it like your future depends on it.

Because it does.

Think about why people stay in toxic jobs they hate

Comfort.

Predictability.

Fear of losing security.

Comfort is a prison dressed up as safety.

The same thing happens in content creation. Creators get comfortable with easy money. They say yes too often. They compromise a little. Then a little more. Until one day, they wake up and no longer recognize their own voice.

They lose their soul trying to gain the world.

And in the end, they lose both.

How Creators Lose Themselves

It never happens overnight.

Losing yourself is quiet. Incremental. Death by a thousand small decisions.

Creators lose themselves when they create for brands instead of people.

When relevance matters more than resonance.

When trends matter more than truth.

When views matter more than values.

When money becomes louder than meaning.

Why Creators Burn Out (and Why I'm Still Here)

When a persona replaces a human.

The saddest part is this: most creators do not realize they are lost until the passion is gone. Until the content feels hollow. Until the burnout becomes unbearable. Until the audience disconnects because the creator disconnected first.

Do not let that be you.

Let me speak as a recipe content creator for a second. I always ask myself, why do so many food creators get stuck?

Most of them keep recycling the same recipe again and again.

Same butter cake. Same mug brownies. Same garlic fried rice. Same chocolate chip cookies. They post it, repost it, and then repost the same thing months later like it is brand new.

That is not growth. That is comfort. And comfort is a creative coffin.

Food is infinite.

From restaurants to eateries, from Michelin counters to grandma kitchens, dishes, desserts, cakes and drinks form a bottomless world of possibilities.

You could explore a new dish every day for the next fifty years and still never reach the edge.

Yet creators recycle because they are scared to explore.

Then what happens? They burn out.

They complain about the algorithm.

They disappear.

Especially the food reviewers, the ones who only eat and point a camera.

But here is the funny part. They do not have to disappear.

They could evolve.

If you can review food, you can learn to cook food.

If you can record a restaurant, you can record a kitchen.

If you learned video editing, you can monetize editing.

If you love restaurants, go review Michelin spots around the world with honesty rather than because someone paid you to act excited.

There are endless creative detours, but most people do not take even one.

And that is just food.

Look at how absurdly large the opportunity gets with something as simple as apples.

If apples are your obsession, you could build content around nothing but apples.

There are hundreds of apple varieties. Most people only know three.

You could document trying every variety.

You could visit orchards and show how apples grow, how they are cultivated and harvested, how climate changes flavor.

You could make apple dishes from Japan, France, Turkey, China and anywhere else.

You could compare apple juices and talk about fructose. You could examine whether juicing is even healthy.

You could dive into apple cider vinegar, fermentation and probiotics.

That is one fruit. One ingredient.

And look how deep the rabbit hole goes.

Most creators are not out of ideas.

They are trapped in their comfort zones.

Curiosity creates content.

Comfort kills it.

Reinvention is not running away from your niche. It is expanding your curiosity inside it. The world is huge, ideas are endless, and if you stay curious, you will never run out of roads to walk.

How to Choose the Right Collaborations

Choosing the right collaborations is not about income. It is about alignment.

Use this filter every time.

Would you use it if they did not pay you?

If not, reject it.

Would you recommend it to your closest friend?

If you hesitate, walk away.

Does it align with your purpose and values?

If your content is about mindful cooking, do not promote junk.

If your platform is about simplicity, do not promote excess.

Does the brand respect your voice?

If they send scripts, talking points, or demand control, run.

Does it pass the ten-year test?

Will you be proud of this decision a decade from now?

Would your future self thank you or resent you?

Short-term money fades.

Long-term reputation compounds.

Reinvention Without Selling Out

Reinvention is not betrayal.

Drift is.

Reinvention is intentional.

Drift is reactive.

You can reinvent your style.

Your format.

Your storytelling.

Your platforms.

Your skills.

But do not reinvent your values.

Reinvent the surface.

Protect the core.

One day, platforms will change.

Numbers will fluctuate.

Offers will dry up.

But the only thing that will still follow you is your name.

And once that name means something real, do not trade it for convenience.

Because finding yourself again after losing your soul is far harder than protecting it in the first place.

Chapter 8

The Power of Gratitude

———————————————

Most motivational speakers talk about gratitude like it is a morning routine checklist.

Wake up. Say thank you. Write three things you are grateful for. Meditate. Drink lemon water. Journal. Manifest. Repeat.

It sounds good.

It looks good on Instagram, TikTok, Snap, and YouTube Shorts.

But that is not what I am talking about here.

I am talking about something deeper. Something harder.

I am talking about learning to find the good even when everything is going wrong.

Not gratitude when life is smooth.

Gratitude when life is messy.

Gratitude when life is unfair.

Gratitude when you are pissed off, tired, disappointed, or defeated.

Anyone can feel good when they are healthy.

When the bills are paid.

When the fridge is full.

When the body is strong.

When relationships are calm.

When nothing is urgently wrong.

That version of gratitude is easy.

It requires no resilience.

No perspective.

No inner work.

The real test comes when your body hurts.

When money is tight.

When stress piles up.

When plans fall apart.

When you are tired, sick, overwhelmed, or scared.

That is where gratitude stops being a feeling and starts becoming a skill.

That kind of gratitude takes strength.

That kind of gratitude takes practice.

That kind of gratitude takes humility.

And it took me years to learn it.

Take something as small as dropping a jar of garlic. It sounds trivial. But in a creator's kitchen, that is a nightmare.

I was preparing a recipe.

The skillet was heating.

The camera was ready.

The mise en place was done.

Then the jar slipped.

It shattered.

Garlic flew everywhere.

My first reaction was the same as anyone's.

Swearing.

Frustration.

Annoyance.

Anger.

Who wouldn't be upset?

But after five seconds, I stopped.

I took a breath.

And I forced myself to look for the good.

Yes, to look for the good in a broken jar of garlic.

And I found it.

Some of the garlic had actually gone bad.

If I had not dropped the jar, I would never have noticed.

I would have cooked with it.

Filmed with it.

Served it.

Wasted even more time and ingredients.

The mistake saved me from a bigger mistake.

The broken jar revealed what needed to be thrown away.

That is the kind of gratitude I am talking about.

Another time, I was making meringue for my daughter's chocolate cloud cake on her birthday.

You know how delicate meringue is.

The timing.

The air.

The stiffness.

The patience.

I whipped four egg whites with 100g of sugar.

Collapse.

I tried again.

Collapse.

Frustration hit hard.

I felt useless.

I felt helpless.

I felt like I had failed my daughter.

Then I stopped and asked myself, what am I missing?

The eggs were old.

Weeks old.

If I had forced it and continued, I would have fed my daughter a cake made from stale eggs.

The failure protected me.

I bought fresh eggs.

The meringue worked perfectly.

Again, gratitude in disguise.

The good hiding inside the bad.

This chapter is not about being grateful only when life behaves.

Anyone can do that.

This chapter is about being grateful when things fall apart.

When plans go wrong.

When mistakes pile up.

When life betrays your expectations.

When you trip over your own feet.

This is gratitude that is earned, not gifted.

Most people think gratitude is about saying thank you.

No.

Gratitude is also about seeing clearly.

It is about training perspective like a muscle.

It is about choosing how to interpret what happens to you.

Jocko Willink said it best: Good.

Something bad happens. Good.

Something fails. Good.

Something breaks. Good.

Now you learn.

Now you adapt.

Now you grow.

This mindset is not denial.

Why Creators Burn Out (and Why I'm Still Here)

It is discipline.

It is ownership.

It is accountability.

Gratitude is not pretending nothing hurts.

Gratitude is refusing to let pain be wasted.

What most people miss is that gratitude is not passive.

It is active interpretation.

The same event can either break you or sharpen you.

The difference is not luck.

The difference is how you frame it in your mind.

Two people can fail at the same thing.

One becomes bitter.

The other becomes better.

Gratitude is the fork in that road.

Gratitude is the point where the road splits:

One direction leads to resentment, the other to growth.

Gratitude is not weakness.

Gratitude is power.

The power to remain calm when others panic.

The power to focus on progress instead of problems.

The power to stay moving when others quit.

Anyone can be grateful when life is beautiful.

Champions are grateful when life misbehaves.

Why Creators Burn Out (and Why I'm Still Here)

When you learn to find the good, everything becomes lighter.

Not because life gets easier, but because you get stronger.

A mistake becomes data.

A failed recipe becomes a lesson.

A bad recording day becomes practice.

A negative comment becomes perspective.

A slow growth month becomes patience training.

Gratitude rewires the mind.

It removes ego.

It lowers anxiety.

It brings clarity.

And most importantly, it keeps you in the game.

Most people want life to go smoothly so they can be grateful.

But life does not work that way.

Life is unpredictable.

Life is unfair.

Life does not care about your plans.

But life rewards adaptation.

Life rewards perspective.

Life rewards those who learn to see opportunity inside chaos.

Gratitude is not pretending everything is okay.

It is trusting that you can still move forward even when it is not.

If your content flops, good. You learned something.

Why Creators Burn Out (and Why I'm Still Here)

If nobody watches, good. You are building muscle.

If your camera fails, good. You will prepare better next time.

If your plans collapse, good. Now you know how to rebuild.

Nothing is wasted if you learn from it.

Nothing is meaningless if you grow from it.

That is the real power of gratitude.

Not the fluffy version.

Not the Instagram-ready version.

Not the cliché version.

The real version is gritty.

Uncomfortable.

Demanding.

It asks you to pause.

To breathe.

To choose perspective when emotion wants control.

So, the next time something goes wrong, pause for five seconds.

Just five.

Take a breath.

And ask yourself:

Where is the good hiding in this?

What is this teaching me?

What is this protecting me from?

What is this preparing me for?

Gratitude is not magic.

Gratitude is training.

And when trained daily, it becomes unshakeable strength.

Think of life like a cup you accidentally drop.

It cracks.

Maybe chips at the rim.

Most people look at it and say:

"It's ruined."

"Throw it away."

But in Japan, there is an art called kintsugi.

Broken pottery is repaired with gold.

The cracks are not hidden.

They are highlighted.

The damage becomes the beauty.

That is what gratitude does.

It does not erase the cracks.

It fills them with meaning.

It reminds you that you are not fragile.

You are repairable.

Rebuildable.

Stronger with every crack you survive.

Your life will break in places.

And once you learn to see the gold in the cracks, you stop fearing the fall.

Gratitude is what turns those cracks into art.

Chapter 9

Sustainable Creation: Lessons from Food

Most people think content creation is a race.

I see it as cooking and baking.

Some dishes take five minutes.

Some take five hours.

And some, the best ones, take days.

This chapter is about the long game. The kind of creative life that doesn't burn you out or break you, but sustains you for decades. The kind that feeds you instead of drains you. And the kind that lasts even when the excitement fades, when the numbers stay small.

Because if there's anything my journey proves, it's this:

Sustainable creation is not built on hype. It's built on purpose.

VLC Media Player didn't last because it was loud; it lasted because it was useful, honest, and never betrayed the people who trusted it.

Why I'm Still Here (When Almost Everyone Else Quit):

By now, you already know I'm a food content creator.

But what you might not know is this:

Most of the people who started in my era, the recipe creators, the home cooks, the bakers, the IG food people, they're gone. Deleted their accounts. Stopped posting. Got tired. Got discouraged. Got burnt out.

Only a handful are still here.

So why am I still here?

Is it because I'm more talented?

No.

More equipped?

Definitely no.

Luckier?

Absolutely not.

I'm still here because my purpose is bigger than me.

My purpose is higher than views, likes, comments, or follower count.

My purpose is higher than brand deals, algorithms, and social media trends.

My purpose is higher than money, materials, or fame.

I didn't start this journey for claps.

I started because I am trying to get more people into the kitchen, cooking and baking.

That's it.

That's the whole story.

That's the whole engine behind Fat Dough.

If one person makes one dish because of something I posted, that's enough for me. That makes me happy. That excites me.

And that's why I'm still here.

11 Years. 10k Followers. Zero Ads. Still Going.

I started in 2014 with fewer than 10 people on my Facebook friends list.

I didn't own a smartphone; I was using a 5-year-old Blackberry.

My website today? Almost no traffic.

My Instagram today? Around 10k.

TikTok? Around 10k.

YouTube? Not even 4k subscribers.

And my entire website?

No ads.

Zero revenue.

No passive income.

No monetization.

99% of people would have quit.

But guess what?

I'm still here.

I still post.

I still create.

I still experiment.

I still share.

Why?

Because I'm not here for the numbers.

I'm here for the small group of people who actually care.

Serve the audience you have, not the audience you wish you had.

That's how you survive long-term.

The Real Question You Must Answer:

What are you willing to do for free for years and years and years?

Not for fame.

Not for money.

Not for applause.

Not for validation.

Not for sponsorships.

But simply because you can't not do it?

For me, it's food.

The idea that Malaysia alone has millions of dishes waiting to be explored excites the shit out of me.

The idea that I can share them and let people expand their palate, that's the fire.

The idea that I can inspire people to cook or bake at home, that's the fuel.

So, ask yourself:

What makes your heart race?

What makes your eyes glow?

What makes you obsessed?

Obsession > Passion

Drive > Motivation

Passion fades when it gets inconvenient.

Obsession doesn't.

Obsession is losing sleep because your mind won't let go.

It's waking up already thinking about the work.

It's creating in silence, long before applause arrives.

Motivation depends on feeling good.

Drive depends on knowing why you're doing this.

Motivation asks, "Do I feel like it today?"

Drive asks, "Does this matter enough to continue?"

That's the truth.

Why Sustainable Creation Matters:

Most creators fail not because they lack talent, but because their creative life is unsustainable.

They quit their jobs too early.

They rely on content for income too fast.

They take brand deals that don't align with their values.

They post for the algorithm instead of their audience.

They chase trends instead of purpose.

That's how burnout happens.

That's how resentment develops.

That's how creators lose themselves.

You want true creative peace?

Keep your job.

Your job pays for this journey.

Your job gives you stability.

Your job gives you breathing room.

Your job gives you freedom to create without desperation.

If you hate your job, get another one.

But don't quit to chase likes.

Let your job fund your dream.

That's what sustainable creation looks like.

I Started With Nothing, And You Can Too:

I started with:

- Zero equipment

- A cheap phone

- Natural lighting

- No editing skills

- No website knowledge

- No SEO knowledge

- No Pinterest knowledge

- No YouTube skills

- No mentors

- No confidence

- Zero fucks given about people's opinions

And somehow… I'm still here.

I learned everything from scratch.

Don't know how to edit photos?

Watch YouTube. Learn. Practice.

Don't know how to make videos?

Watch YouTube. Learn. Practice.

Don't know SEO?

Ask someone. Or Google. Or ChatGPT.

Don't know Pinterest?

My youngest daughter taught me.

When you stop learning, you stop growing.

When you stop growing, you die creatively.

Use what you have.

Start where you are.

Act with what you know.

The rest, you will learn along the way.

My System: How I Actually Do This While Working Full-Time:

People assume I'm full-time.

Nope.

I'm a full-time employee.

A full-time single parent.

And still a full-time creator.

How?

I plan my recipes monthly.

I cook/bake and shoot on weekends.

Why Creators Burn Out (and Why I'm Still Here)

I edit photos on the bus ride to work.

I write blog posts after dinner.

I edit videos whenever I can steal pockets of time.

I even skip lunch sometimes to work on my content.

Because I value time over money.

And I value meaning over comfort.

You'll be shocked how much you can accomplish when you stop waiting for perfect conditions.

The World Is Bigger Than You Think, Even If Your Niche Is "Small":

People laugh when I say things like:

"You can make content about Ninja Turtles."

"You can make content about spreadsheets."

"You can make content about paper airplanes."

But it's true.

There's a legit paper airplane world championship.

People train for it.

People study aerodynamics for it.

People build communities around it.

If spreadsheets excite you, do spreadsheets.

If manga excites you, do manga.

If coffee excites you, do coffee.

If sneakers excite you, do sneakers.

If Ninja Turtles excite you, I'll subscribe.

There are no "boring" niches.

Only boring creators.

The moment you're excited, your audience can feel it.

And excitement is contagious.

Sustainable Creation Is the Only Creation That Lasts:

You can burn bright.

Or you can burn long.

But you cannot burn both bright and long at the same time.

Choose long.

Choose slow.

Choose intentional.

Choose meaningful.

And ask yourself every single day:

Have I grown today?

Have I learned today?

Have I improved today?

Have I created something today?

Little by little.

Step by step.

Brick by brick.

This is how you build a legacy.

My Lessons. Now What About You?

I've shared my truth.

I've shown you the behind-the-scenes.

I've told you the ugly parts and the beautiful parts.

I've walked you through the mindset, the grind, the burnout, the obsession, the purpose.

Now it's your turn to answer:

What excites the shit out of you?

What would you do for free?

What are you willing to stick with for 10 years?

What do you want to give the world?

What do you want your audience to feel?

What legacy are you building?

Because sustainable creation isn't a strategy.

It's a way of life.

And if I, a tired, broke, gout-ridden single father with a day job, can build something, so can you.

If you've made it all the way here, that tells me something important about you.

It tells me you're not just curious. You're serious.

It tells me there's something inside you that refuses to stay quiet.

It tells me you're hungry for more than the life you're living right now.

And above all, it tells me you're ready.

Not ready in the sense of "perfect." Nobody is perfect.

Not ready in the sense of "fully equipped." Nobody starts fully equipped.

Not ready in the sense of "confident." Confidence comes after the doing, not before.

I mean ready in the simplest, most honest way:

You wouldn't be holding this book if a part of you didn't believe there's more in you.

So, here's what I want you to know:

You don't need permission.

You don't need validation.

You don't need the algorithm to love you.

You don't need the world to understand you.

All you need is one tiny decision: Start.

Start with what you have.

Start with where you are.

Start with the tools you already own.

Start with the imperfect ideas in your head.

Start even if you're scared.

Start even if you're tired.

Start even if nobody believes in you yet.

Because the truth is, nobody will believe in you until you give them a reason to.

And that reason begins with your first step.

Why Creators Burn Out (and Why I'm Still Here)

This journey will challenge you.

It will frustrate you.

It will humble you.

But it will also grow you in ways you cannot imagine.

One day, you're going to look back at this exact moment, you reading these words, and say:

"That's where everything changed."

Not because the world changed.

But because you did.

So, here's my last message to you:

We have already won the biggest lottery there is. We are the ones who get to die knowing that we have lived. The number of people who could have existed but never did is unimaginably vast, exponentially, absurdly large. Trillions of possible lives that never got the chance to breathe, to feel, to love, to wonder. And yet here we are, spinning through this vast universe on a pale blue dot, conscious enough to create meaning where there was none. We are the ones who brought meaning to our solar system, and perhaps, in our own quiet way, to the galaxy.

You do not owe the world perfection.

You owe it your presence.

You are capable.

You are resilient.

You are built for this.

And whatever dream you're holding in your chest... it deserves to be real.

Now close this book.

And go create something.

Go build something.

Go share something.

Go tell your story.

The world may not know your name yet.

But it will.

Keep going.

I'm rooting for you.

Put down this book.

Go live.

Go make the rest of your life the best of your life.

Made in the USA
Middletown, DE
13 January 2026

26817516R00059